# Acing the Interview

## Playing Your Best Hand When It Counts*!*

**Multi-award Winning and Nationally Recognized Headhunter**

# Sandy Scardino

### Reveals *Her* Secrets to *Your* Success*!*

"…if you prepare using her time tested exercises, you will position yourself ahead of the crowd."
Mike Menotti
Corporate Recruiting Manager

**Outskirts Press, Inc.**
**Denver, Colorado**

Acing the Interview
Playing Your Best Hand When It Counts!
All Rights Reserved.
Copyright © 2009 Sandy Scardino
V2.0

Cover Photo © 2009 iStockphoto.com/Anton Prado. All rights reserved - used with permission.

Outskirts Press, Inc.
http://www.outskirtspress.com

ISBN: 978-1-4327-2374-3

Library of Congress Control Number: 2009924072

Outskirts Press and the "OP" logo are trademarks belonging to Outskirts Press, Inc.

PRINTED IN THE UNITED STATES OF AMERICA

# What Industry Experts Are Saying...

"Acing the Interview is the most comprehensive guide to successful interviewing that I've seen. It contains excellent techniques and tools that, when used, will differentiate a candidate from the competition--I know this to be true from experience. Sandy covers all facets of the interview process and takes the reader step-by-step through the do's and don'ts of the interview process. Nothing is left to "guess work"...it's all there in black and white. This is a must read for anyone serious about winning the interview."

Craig Boulet, President
Cornerstone Resource Group
www.cornerstoneresource.net

"Clearly, job seekers are facing more and more competition in a tighter and tighter market. To make themselves stand out, they need to go in well-prepared for every interview, with ready answers for the most difficult questions that might be thrown at them. This is a must!

Sandy's book takes readers through the entire process. The book prepares candidates to "ace" the job interview with first hand knowledge from an expert in the field. Sandy understands the crucial examination of today's hiring authority, their competition, and the techniques candidates need to know to get their foot in the door. Readers will learn the basic questions employers will typically ask, along with a lot more that they never expected, most importantly, the guidance on how to answer each of them. In addition, the book includes essential questions applicants should be asking those on the other side of the desk. This book is a professional guideline to getting the job"

Derrick Green
President and CEO
The JAG Group
Healthcare Specialists
www.thejaggroup.com

"Finally! An actual professional with real world interviewing skills has taken the time to share her trade secrets and explain the difference between the Theory and Reality of getting a job. If you are looking for needless stats and feel good rhetoric, this book is not for you. This workbook is written in plain English, with one goal in mind – making you the candidate best prepared to get the job.

Whether you are interviewing for a call center job or a senior management role, if you prepare using her time tested exercises, you will position yourself ahead of the crowd."

Mike Menotti
Corporate Recruiting Manager
Exterran Energy Solutions

"Throw out everything you think you know about interviewing and read this book! Sandy has the most successful interview to offer ratio I've ever seen. You can succeed in every type of interview for every type of position using her approach."

Donya Davis Jones, Principal
Donya Rhea Consulting
Recruiting & Staffing Specialists
www.donyarhea.com

"Being in the national recruitment industry since 1980, I have observed that many professionals are ill-prepared for the interview and receive advice on the subject from all the wrong people-relatives, academics, strangers they meet on buses. That's why it's imperative for professionals to completely digest every word Sandy shares with them on this subject. She has been on the "firing line" in the market, where the interview is the most important tool used to both advance the career and evaluate talent. I'd recommend this to anyone who has a career-whether you're "looking", hiring or just want to maintain a healthy career path."

Michael Goldman, CPC
Founder and President
Strategic Associates, Inc.
www.strategicassociates.com
The Pinnacle Society, Founding Member
and Past President
A consortium of 75 of the top recruiters
in the U.S.
www.pinnaclesociety.org

"Take her advice, prepare as she says and you'll likely get the offer. I saw her make offers happen for her candidates through these methods consistently, time after time. They were often not the most qualified; they were, quite simply, prepared to shine above the others."

Emma Jacobs Woerner
Founder and President
Emjay Computer Careers
Past Pinnacle Society Member

# A Word of Thanks...

The place to start with the thank-yous is always with my amazing children. You are quite literally the reason I get up each morning and what I give thanks for each night. You have been patient when I was busy working and supportive during difficult times. You are great business partners who inspire and challenge me. I am forever grateful I have been given the privilege of being your mother. I love you more than you can ever know. Thanks also, for my precious grandkids, the ones already here and those yet to come!

Thanks to Emma for her innate ability to recognize a silk purse when she sees one, even if it's temporarily disguised as a sow's ear! Thanks for the great opportunity, the great training and the great times we had at Emjay. We worked as hard as we played and played as hard as we worked. I had the time of my life!

Big sister Gail, thanks for showing me the ropes and making me plant plastic flowers in the rain; most of all thanks for sharing your can of tuna each day before I could afford to buy lunch! Lastly, thanks for constantly telling me to store up for winter; that lesson served me well.

Thanks to all the wild and crazy people I met and worked with during my years headhunting. I learned something from each and every one of you. Thanks especially to Mikey, Donya and Derrick for keeping the friendship alive so many years after we worked together. You mean the world to me.

Mike, thanks for being my content editor; you really helped me take it up a notch and all for the price of a home cooked meal and a good bottle of wine!

Sheri, thanks for your great suggestions and help editing and proofing. It was a tremendous help. You are also a terrific game partner; I'm up for another game of Cranium in Hawaii any time you are!

Theus, my technical genius, you have built last minute web sites for me, recovered lost data that others couldn't recover and helped me load my parent's furniture into a moving van. You are like another one of my kids. Thank you for all of that!

Betsy, thanks for the loan of the clothes, what a sport you were. You really helped me get back up on my feet at a most difficult time – thank you for that as well.

To the many people in my circle of friends, both old and new, who have cheered me up, cheered me on and supported me in a multitude of ways - a heartfelt thanks to each and every one of you.

With gratitude,

Sandy

# Table of Contents

# The First Impression

**B**efore getting in to the preparation process portion of how to ace your interview, I want to address the first impression. The importance of the first impression cannot be overstated. The first impression won't assure that you *will* get the position, *but it can most certainly assure that you won't if it is negative in any way*. The average number of seconds it takes to make a first impression according to psychologists who study these things, is about 20 to 25 seconds. Most say about 17 seconds. 17 seconds! A rare few out there say between 30 and 60 seconds. There do not seem to be ANY opinions that state that first impressions could take longer to form than 60 seconds. That impression is then so far imbedded in to the interviewer's mind at a subconscious level, that it more than likely may never be reversed. Never! That is because the first impression is an impression of the senses. Senses go beyond logic or fact.

Let's say that those rare few psychologists who say it takes as long as 30-60 seconds are correct; that a decision about you is formed in 60 seconds tops. That being true, do you really think that the first impression is not as important as the rest of the interview? Think again. You *must* take the first impression seriously. That's why I'm addressing it first!

Let's go through the five senses to understand how to make the best first impression when meeting potential employers.

<u>Visual Sense</u>: How do you look? Are you appropriately dressed for the interview? What is appropriate dress for an interview? Do you need a haircut? A shave? Is there a spot on your tie? Is there a stain on your skirt?

You want to look sharp when your potential employer first lays eyes on you. Have an interview suit and a back-up for a second interview. If you are applying for a position that doesn't require a suit, it doesn't matter; wear a suit to the interview. If the potential employer says you don't' have to dress up for the interview, it doesn't matter; wear a suit to the interview.

Borrow clothes if you have to. I still remember my interview with the head-hunting firm that I worked for. I went to the first interview in borrowed clothes. I went to the second interview in borrowed clothes. I started my new career in borrowed clothes. In fact, the only person I knew who had appropriate clothes for me to borrow that would fit me, was my soon to be ex-husband's first wife! I thought she was such a sport to loan me clothes. This is no time to be too proud to do what needs to be done to secure a future. Within three years of borrowing those clothes, I was making a very nice six figure income. Was swallowing my pride to borrow the right clothes worth it? You betcha!

<u>Sense of Touch/Feel</u>: How does this apply to an interview? This sense is twofold; touch and feel. The sense of 'touch' applies predominately to the handshake. In my ten years as a headhunter, I felt that the handshake was so important, that if someone did not give me a firm handshake when I met them, I addressed it immediately. I had them re-shake my hand until we got a firm (not TOO firm,

it's not a contest) handshake. Grip the other person's hand firmly letting the 'v' between your thumb and forefinger interlock with the 'v' between their thumb and forefinger and wrap your fingers around their hand. You will find that a handshake usually consists of two or three downward motions before letting go of the grip. Practice this with someone who has a comfortable and confident handshake. Ladies, this applies to you as well; maybe even more so. Confidence in someone is not gained by getting a 'wet noodle' handshake from them. Quite the opposite, so don't underestimate this.

The sense of "feel" has to do with emotions or feelings. It is important that you create a rapport with the interviewer. By this point, you will have done your research on both the company and the interviewer. As you enter the interviewer's office, glance around the room for something you may have in common or that you can comment on. Is there a diploma from a college/university that you know something about? Did you, a parent or sibling attend that school? Do you like their football team? Comment on that. Is there a picture of the person's family? In a sail boat? On a hike? At Disneyworld? Is there a point of reference that you can make with any one of these things? Even just the comment 'I've always wanted to learn to sail' (referring to the picture) is enough of an ice breaker to give a more relaxed tone to the meeting. It sounds simple; it is. Effectively building rapport is important. People hire people who are qualified, but in the case of equal qualifications, people hire who they like. Most people like friendly people. Remember, you don't have to be stone-faced or dull to be professional. Professionals are people, too.

The sense of smell: This is a sense you don't want to stir up in the interview – in more than one way. I'll explain. A shower should be the starting point of getting ready for the interview. Also, make sure that your clothing is freshly cleaned or washed. Smell your clothes before you put them on. Check your breath; ask a friend, sibling or spouse to give you a check on that if you can't tell.

You want to smell fresh, but you don't want to overdo, or even 'do' the cologne thing. Say you want to ignore this piece of advice. Say you think you know the exact amount of cologne to put on so as to not move in to the 'overdoing it' category. You walk in to the interview, feeling good about your lightly scented self and you don't get the job. I had a hiring manager who eventually confessed to me that he didn't hire someone because they wore the same cologne that his ex-spouse wore. (He had just finished a very bitter divorce) Do you really want to take that chance? The best cologne in the interview is no cologne in the interview.

If you smoke, DON'T SMOKE AFTER YOU DRESS FOR YOUR INTERVIEW. Trust me when I tell you that the smell of smoke lingers on you and your clothing. I used to smoke. I smoked for many years. Shortly after I quit smoking I was on an elevator and the doors began to close when a woman popped in at the last minute and the smell of cigarette smoke hit me like a ton of bricks. I found out that cigarette smoke is much more detectible to a non-smoker. I never knew I smelled that bad. Even though quitting was a personal health decision, I will never forget thinking that I never wanted to smell like that again. Just like cologne, the smell of cigarette smoke can be offensive, too, and is easily detected.

The sense of taste: How would this possibly apply? There are times when the interview will take place off of the company site…at a restaurant. Order food that is easy to eat without making a mess. Don't order spaghetti that may slop on to your shirt or bar-b-cue ribs that will get your hands, face and teeth sticky and messy. Corn on the cob may get stuck in your teeth. It's distracting to sit across from someone with corn in their teeth. Yes, anything can make a mess; just remember that some things are less likely to make a mess. Don't forget that some foods are more likely to cause gas and/or bad breath. Stay away from garlic and uncooked onions so your breath won't smell of them.

Never, under any circumstances, order an alcoholic beverage, even if the person or persons you are meeting with order one. Politely turn down the offer if asked. If there is such an insistence that you order one that you feel pressured to do so, take a sip when it is set at the table, then ignore it and don't take more than another small sip or two during the entire meal. Don't let yourself get relaxed enough to say something stupid.

You just know when a hiring manager calls you with the initial interview feedback "I guess we shouldn't have offered him a drink at dinner" that the conversation is going to go downhill sharply from there. It seems that my candidate had a drink and felt relaxed enough to share TMI (too much information) about his girlfriend who lived in another city and was trying to get him to move to be with her. After his second drink he got "a little misty eyed" about it and said he really wanted to be with her and she wouldn't move to be with him. He talked about the dilemma he faced in trying to decide whether to move or risk losing her.

He wasn't hired. It's not that we don't all have 'human' situations in our lives. Sharing them isn't always appropriate. It doesn't take much alcohol to make saying or doing something stupid sound like a good idea. If there is such an insistence that you take a drink, maybe this isn't the right company for you. If you can't resist the drink, maybe you should be at a different meeting.

The sense of sound/hearing: Be cognizant of your tone/pitch, your volume and your inflections. Be sure your voice is friendly AND confident. But not so confident that you sound cocky. We will talk about WHAT you say and HOW you phrase it later. This is about the way your voice sounds. Speak loudly and clearly enough to be heard. Don't shout. If the interviewer is leaning forward and squinting, it may be that he can't hear you very well. Just be aware of how you sound, whether you tape record yourself and listen, or ask a friend to critique you.

Your voice becomes even more important when you do a phone interview. Ask someone how you come across on the phone. Are you too loud? Too soft spoken? Do you tend to interrupt the person you are talking to when you're on the phone? Ask someone you talk to by phone often to critique you honestly.

This next item doesn't fall under any particular sense, perhaps common sense, but it is a MUST mention. Do not, under any circumstances, go in to an interview with ANY electronic device that will ring, beep, vibrate or otherwise distract you in any way. It is also just about the rudest thing can happen while you are in an interview. It says to the potential employer, "Even though I'm here in the interview with you, it's not the most important thing to me right now." Whatever it is it can wait until you are finished with your interview.

# Resumes and Cover Letters

T think of your resume as your calling card. It is used to entice the company to bring you in for an interview. Generally, the farther back in to your background that you go, the less detailed information you need to put on your resume. In other words, a potential employer is more interested in what you have done in the last five years than what you did ten years ago. The exception would be if what you did ten years ago is pertinent to the position you are seeking. In that case, give more detail on positions you held that apply to the job you are seeking.

There are two basic styles of resumes. The first style is chronological; on this style put your experience in reverse chronological order starting with your most recent position. The second is called a functional resume; it highlights your talents and skills in categories without any chronological order. So it may have sections for technical skills, accounting package conversions, project leader responsibilities etc. People with choppy work histories tend to use functional resumes. I have always preferred the chronological resumes because I could tell at a glance what skills were current and if not current, when they were last used. I have found chronological resumes to be the preferred resumes of companies for the same reason.

Many companies do Key Word Searches when going through resumes. They electronically scan resumes and if they are looking for someone with specific experience like Peachtree accounting software or Windows NT operating systems, they will do a key word search of the resumes they receive. Be sure to include the 'buzz words' in the body of your resume so your resume is picked up on any electronic searches for your skill set.

Cover letters are NOT your work history or your life story. They should be short and concise. They simply introduce you and offer your resume to be considered for the position. Cover letters should go something like this…

*Dear Hiring Manager,*

*Enclosed please find my resume in consideration for the Project Leader's position in your accounting department.*

*I feel that my past experience delivering projects on time and under budget, coupled with my enthusiasm for leading a team to project completion makes me a perfect candidate for your open Project Leader's position.*

*I will contact you on Friday to set an interview at your earliest convenience. Feel free to contact me sooner if an earlier interview is desired.*

*Thank you for your consideration,*

*Perfect Candidate*

Don't get in to your background in detail in the cover letter. It is simply a request for an interview. Take it from someone who read resumes and cover letters daily for ten years, there are turn offs and turn ons with resumes and cover letters. Lengthy, wordy cover letters don't always get read. Your background goes on your resume, not in your cover letter. Keep it simple.

# The Interviewer, Application Forms and References

Most people aren't professional interviewers. Even most human resource people aren't really professional interviewers. Most hiring authorities are somewhat nervous about choosing the right person to fill the position. There is always the anxiety that they may choose incorrectly and will look bad in their boss's eyes. If they are the boss, they are worried about choosing the wrong person; it is expensive to hire the wrong person. Most people sitting on the other side of the desk during ANY interview would be happy if you just sat down and matched your skills to their needs without much effort on their part. They know they are supposed to get certain information from you. They know they are trying to determine if you know what you need to know to perform the job. Most really aren't that skilled at matching that up and would much rather be doing their job. This is why you will do what you can to put them at their ease and develop a rapport as shown in the previous section AND take control of the interview as outlined in the section on controlling the interview.

You may also interview with someone from the human resource department. The amount of input that your human resource interview will have varies greatly from company to company. Generally speaking, they have less input in terms of qualifying you than the manager from the actual department you will be working in. Sometimes you will have to interview with a human resource person who is at a more junior level than you. Just be polite and answer the questions so you can move on to the department interview.

You may interview with different levels in the department as well as people in other departments. Peer interviews are usually about chemistry. Gain rapport with potential peers. Find common ground. Peers recommend who they want to work with on a day to day basis.

No matter who it is that you are interviewing with, if they ask you to fill out an application form – *fill it out!* It speaks volumes in terms of your ability to cooperate. I've had people come in to interview with me and when asked by the receptionist to fill out an application form, they refused because they had already provided their resume. I would go in to the lobby and politely explain why I needed them to fill out the form. If they still balked about filling it out, I would let them know that I now did, in fact, have all of the information I needed on them and thanked them for coming in for the interviw. Some would say that they would fill out an application on the "real interview". I let them know that this *was* the real interview and they would not be moving on to interview with my client. I don't care if you are interviewing to be a ditch digger or a CEO, don't be perceived as being uncooperative by refusing to fill out an application form. *Fill it out completely.* If the job doesn't mean enough to you to fill out an application form, don't go to the interview.

When placing references on application forms, there may be a box to check saying it is OK to check references. Be sure to check this unless your references are people who you work with currently who don't know you are looking for a job. Most large companies with HR departments will only check dates, eligibility for rehire and salary information to operate within the bounds of legality. If you don't check the box, be prepared to show other documentation to confirm employment dates and salary.

Back door references or relationship references are checked quite often. You simply call someone who you know worked at a company with the person you are considering hiring. These are more often than not, people who aren't even on your list of references. It usually starts with something like "Between you and me, what was Joe Schmoe really like to work with?" or "Off the record, was Joe proficient in his 'abc' skills?"

If you want to know what your references are going to say about you, ask them. You will want to ask if you can use them anyway, so just throw in "what will you say when asked about my job performance and/or skill set?" Without meaning to, some people will say some really unhelpful things when giving a reference on you. I've had to suggest to many candidates to change the list of people on their reference sheet. The reasons vary. Some people were too chatty. Some didn't sound very intelligent. Some got too much in to personal details. Just because you ask someone if you *can* use them doesn't mean you *have* to use them. Find out what they will say before you actually list them as references. It's okay to ask, "Will you highlight my management skills?" or "What will you tell them about my interpersonal skills?"

# Preparation and Interview Skills

Preparing for the interview is done in several stages. Most prep should be done even before an interview is arranged. In fact, it is to your advantage to do the preparation outlined in this section and the next section on a very regular basis while you are working. This exercise also allows you to keep your resume updated easily. A layoff or loss of job is a very emotional time. It can feel and be quite devastating. How much better would you feel at this time if you already had an up to date resume to send out immediately? And can you imagine already having the perfect answer to most of the questions the interviewer will ask? The RAP and PAR exercises described later will not only put you in that position, but it is a natural part of what your resume should consist of.

Too many people think that if they have a clean copy of their resume to give each person they will see during the interview process, they have properly prepared for their interview. Nothing could be further from the truth.

That being said, make sure after the complete preparation that you DO have clean copies of your resume for each person you will see. I recommend that you get one of those portfolios that is a leather or nice vinyl folder that has a legal tablet on the right side and a pocket on the left when it's opened. Put clean copies of your resume in the pocket. Get one with a clamp at the top of the pocket side so your resumes don't flop around when you open it and fold it back under the legal pad side to form a firm writing surface. Again, borrow one or invest in one. It makes a great "lap desk" so you won't be juggling something flimsy to jot notes on.

It is perfectly fine to jot notes in the interview. Have three sections on the page; one across the top for reminders, one for essential points you must cover and one for non essential questions you want answered but will go back to find out later because they have no bearing on matching your experience to the job. The section on essential points will be only for things that trigger the experience in your background that you must let them know you have. In other words, if the hiring manager mentions they are doing a system conversion, simply jot *conversion* in the space you've allotted for this. Items in this space are points that must be covered by you before you leave the interview. This is how you match yourself to the position you are interviewing for. Be sure to scratch through each point as you cover it. If you don't you will find yourself looking at the list trying to decipher what you have covered and what you haven't. There is a sample Interview Note Page outlined on page 45 in the Examples and Exercises section.

In the case of the 'conversion experience', when a break for you to speak next comes in, you would respond with "You mentioned the upcoming conversion. In my last project I was responsible for the analytical team who determined the user's needs for the new accounting system. I met with the lead from the development team and we devised a strategy for information to flow more easily between the two teams, resulting in an on time and under budget project." But it is hard to sound quite so eloquent at the drop of a hat. Or is it?

One of the best techniques I have ever used to help the job candidate was in the form of a simple chart that the candidate filled in. I called it a RAP sheet for two reasons. The main reason was that it stood for **R**ESPONSIBILITY/**A**CTION/**P**AYOFF. The other was just for my own amusement. When I was younger the phrase "Let's rap" meant let's talk, usually referring to an in depth conversation about something. It seemed oddly appropriate for a tool to allow you to talk more intelligently about your own background. But I digress.

Take a sheet of paper and turn it sideways. Draw two lines vertically making three columns. At the top of the first column write the word **R**ESPONSIBILITY; on the top of the second column write the word **A**CTION and on the top of the third column write the word **P**AYOFF.

Now one by one *and on a separate sheet* of paper, list all of your current responsibilities, both large and small. It doesn't matter how seemingly insignificant you think they are, list them on this separate sheet. After you list responsibilities from your current position, go back position by position and list your responsibilities for each position at each company. Continue to do this in reverse chronological order until you've reached the beginning of your work history.

Take your current responsibilities and one at a time place them on your RAP sheet and draw them across the page filling in the ACTION and PAYOFF columns so that they look like the following examples. Each example is for a different position to show how this exercise can apply to various types of jobs.

| RESPONSIBILITY | ACTION | PAYOFF |
|---|---|---|
| Lead a team of analysts to determine user needs and deliver the information to the development team. | Initiated a meeting with the lead from the development team to coordinate efforts and speed up the flow of information between the groups. | The development project came in on time and under budget due to there being no lag time in gathering and delivering user needs to the developers. |
| Development of new clients. | Created an industry newsletter and distributed it among targeted potential and existing clients. | Quickly considered an industry 'expert' because of my editorials in the newsletters. Clients took my calls more readily and tended to do business with me over their other sources. |
| Coordinate schedules for 3 VPs including meetings and travel. | Lined up contacts with several caterers for the meetings and two highly recommended travel agents to handle the travel with a simple phone call. | Even last minute meetings and travel were all able to be handled quickly and with ease. |
| Increase revenues at our retail locations. | Designed a customer survey to determine what additional goods & services they would like to see at our store locations. | Added two products and one service that increased revenues by 15% within the next 6 months. |

Again, go one by one placing your responsibilities on the RAP sheet in reverse chronological order until you've reached the beginning of your work history. Fill in the ACTION and PAYOFF sections as you transfer each RESPONSIBILITY on to the RAP sheet.

Once you've finished this, you are ready to turn each one of these in to a polished sentence that will accurately describe your experience. It allows you to have, at the ready, all of your past experience in a well thought out answer as opposed to reaching in to your memory and having to construct an answer that gives the interviewer a clear depiction of your experience; and coming up with it on the spot and under pressure.

Look at RAP Example #1. Take a minute to read it again. Now for the sentence/answer we make out of it:

*As a team lead for the analyst on our conversion project, I was responsible for making sure 'user needs' information was quickly and accurately provided to the development team. I asked the developer's team lead to meet with me to determine better and faster ways of getting user needs information to his team. As a result, the project came in ahead of time and under budget.*

As you can see, the completed RAP sheet practically writes your answers for you. You use these not only as answers to questions, but also as points you want to make so as to match your skills to the hiring manager's needs.

Now let's look at RAP Example #2 and put it in to sentence/answer form.

*My number one responsibility at ABC Medical Sales was to develop new clients. I decided to take the time to put together an industry newsletter for existing clients AND targeted clients that I wanted to work with. I quickly gained 'expert' status through editorials I wrote for the newsletter. I found that clients took my calls more often and began calling me regularly to discuss industry topics. This lead to a natural shift in our current clients doing more business with us and we gained many of the targeted companies as clients.*

Can you see how you can take your experience and put it across to the hiring authority in a very clear and concise manner? You not only are clear and concise, you show achievement with answers structured as such. Before we go on, take a minute to do a RAP exercise with just one of your background experiences. It can be as simple as buying the paperclips for the company. Listen to the way we can make that sound.

RESPONSIBILITY - Purchasing the paper clips.

ACTION – Searched the internet for bulk rate paper clips. Partnered with the other departments to be able to place the minimum bulk paper clip order.

PAYOFF – Saved 10% on all paper clips purchased and we never ran out of paper clips again.

Sentence/Answer:

*It was one of my responsibilities to purchase the paper clips. I located 2 vendors to work with that were very economical and offered bulk rates. I partnered with the other departments to be able to place the minimum order required for bulk rate orders. As a result we saved 10% on our order and never ran out of paper clips.*

Now turn to the Practice RAP Exercise in the Examples and Exercise section in the back of the book. Take the time now to do this exercise using just one recent or current responsibility. Doing this now will help to clarify in your mind what the RAP sheet is all about; do it now – I'll wait.

See how simple it is? Now, as you find out through the course of your interview what the position requires, you can give a well thought out, intelligent answer that shows a demonstrated ability with proven results.

The RAP sheet is a valuable tool for other things as well. It is a thorough review of your background. If you were going to a meeting to talk about a project, company financial information or any other subject, you would be remiss not to be completely prepared and know your subject matter intimately. Your own background is no different. Have you ever been in an interview, or a simple conversation for that matter, and when it was over and you walked away, thought "I wish I would have remembered to say this or tell them about that". I know I have.

STUDY YOUR RAP SHEET BEFORE EVERY INTERVIEW; and study the sentences/answers that you've constructed out of each of the points on your RAP sheet. Another vital use for your RAP sheet is as a resume creator. I recommend that you prepare a shell or template resume with company names in reverse chronological order, titles that you held and dates you worked at each. Now you can add and subtract your various experience on to and off of your resume at will. This allows you to easily tailor your resume to fit a variety of positions you may want to put yourself forward to. You can look at your RAP sheet and hand pick the experience you want to highlight for each potential position. Then simply transfer it to your "shell" resume under the correct company. Be sure to save each resume so you can use it for similar positions with minimal updating.

Both the RAP sheet and the PAR sheet that we will talk about shortly, are also great tools for performance reviews. They will help you focus on accomplishments and more easily talk about the reasons you deserve that raise, promotion or corner office!

Always keep your RAP and PAR sheets updated. It should be part of the ongoing maintenance of your career. Pick a date such as the 1$^{st}$ or 15$^{th}$ of the month. Maybe you could use your birth date and do it on that day each month. It may be that you review it and nothing has changed. It may be you have just one new responsibility added to your plate with no actions even taken yet, let alone any results. The RAP sheet is easy to maintain at that pace. It becomes more of a project when it is done all at once. That being said, do the project now! Having an updated RAP sheet is more important than keeping your resume updated. It is the tool that you create your resume from, it enables you to speak eloquently about your experience and it allows you to review your background continuously - especially before an interview or performance review.

# Behavioral Based Interviews

What is a behavioral based interview? It is based on the principle that past behavior is the greatest predictor of future behavior. How is this determined in an interview? It goes beyond matching skills and moves in to matching the needed competency that may include those skills. You may not know which type of interview you are going to be faced with, so you'd better be prepared for both. It will usually be the larger and more structured companies that will use behavioral based questions.

At first glance, the types of behavior based questions that are typically asked can be a little intimidating. They include inquiries like, "Tell me about a time when you had to change your point of view to take in to account changing priorities" or "Describe a time when you had to confront your boss on a sensitive issue. How did you handle it?" Or possibly, "Give me an example of a conflict that arose between you and a coworker. How did you resolve it?"

So instead of specific skill questions like, "Can you use the XYZ software?" you might hear the question, "Give an example of how your ability to use the XYZ software was an asset to the department." The answer to the first inquiry would show skill; the answer to the second would show competency. The difference is subtle, but important to know when developing answers to behavior based questions.

Prep for the behavioral interview is almost identical to the prep for the skill side of the interview. In the skill prep, we used a RAP sheet. We are going to spell that backwards now and use a PAR sheet to prepare for the behavioral interview. Think of it as something that will put you 'on par' to get the position. Start with a three column sheet just like the RAP exercise.

PAR stands for **P**ROBLEM or **P**ROFICIENCY/**A**CTION/**R**ESULT, which will be your three column headings. When we started the RAP exercise, we made a list of RESPONSIBILITIES. You will now make a list of past PROBLEMS you have had or PROFICIENCIES (or competencies) that you have demonstrated. Use the list of behavior categories below to seek out situations in your work history that highlight these proficiencies. Be methodical and go back position by position and think about situations you've encountered and compliments you have received based on problems you've solved. This is not a time to skim lightly through your brain; dig deep. Also, go through your resume and your RAP sheet to find situations that demonstrate your proficiencies and put them on this list. These things will more than likely be situational as opposed to skill based.

Now place each PROBLEM/PROFICIENCY on the PAR sheet one at a time and draw it across the page just like you did on the RAP sheet by next telling the ACTION that you used to solve the problem or how you demonstrated a proficiency or competency. Lastly, tell the RESULT of your actions which should include a benefit to your company, department or project.

Using your completed RAP and PAR sheets, go down the list of behavioral categories and one by one see which categories each of the RESPONSIBILITIES on the RAP and PROBLEMS/

PROFICIENCIES on the PAR sheets fit in to. You may be able to find something in each item on your RAP and PAR sheets that demonstrates proficiency in the communication category. Move on to the next category and see how many items fit in to *that* category and so on down the list. Each of the responsibilities may fall in to more than one or many categories. Let's go back to number one on the RAP sheet. It may fit in to all of these categories: Effective Communication, Leadership, Conflict Resolution, Problem Solving/Judgment, Strategic Thinking, and so on.

Concentrate now on *categorizing* each of your RESPONSIBILITIES and PROBLEMS/ PROFICIENCIES as shown above using the list of categories provided below. Each item on your RAP and PAR sheets should end up with several categories 'attached' to it. Really give careful thought to how each would be an example of the category in which it may fall. Remember, each may fall in to many categories. It's too hard to anticipate the exact behavioral question because there are too many possible ways to ask them. If you categorize your past problems and responsibilities and are able to tell the story that shows how you demonstrated the traits that these categories represent, you will be very well prepared for behavioral based questions.

Now take each one of the behavioral categories attached to each item and tailor your responses to fit. Each category may skew the answer in a slightly different direction to highlight that particular proficiency. For simplicity, we will stay with example #1 from the RAP sheet. Under categories such as Communication, Achieves Results, Planning, Problem Solving and the like, you may have as your response, "The project I was assigned to lead had almost come to a halt. I saw that there were difficulties between the two departments in communicating the user needs and turning it in to a usable product. This seemed to be causing some discord between the departments. As the leader of the analytical team, I took the initiative to meet with the leader of the development team to find a better way to 'flow' the information quickly and more accurately. We decided to have a 30 minute breakfast meeting in the conference room on Mondays and Wednesdays to make sure we were all on track and communicating the needs properly. The two teams began to look forward to these meetings. It boosted morale, made their jobs easier and the project began to move much faster. For the cost of a few muffins and a pot of coffee, we finished the project on time and under budget."

Now when asked to show an example of Effective Communication, Leadership, Conflict Resolution, Problem Solving, Judgment or Strategic Thinking, you have one example that may easily fit several categories. It may have also included a scenario in which you had to go to your boss to report an uncooperative employee that he hired, constituting confronting your boss on a sensitive issue. Remember, dig deep!

You will now go back through the PAR and RAP sheets and practice telling, in story form, your 'answer' to some anticipated questions about your competencies. Go through the list of questions I've given you and the list of competencies that companies look for proficiency in. Practice telling the stories. Use your PAR and RAP sheets as a guideline for these stories. I can tell you that your ability to answer questions in a logical, methodical form matters big time. That is worth repeating loudly...YOUR ABILITY TO ANSWER BEHAVIORAL QUESTIONS IN LOGICAL FORM IS ABOUT AS IMPORTANT AS THE ANSWER ITSELF. If you have good information to give them, yet you stammer and stutter trying to put your answer together on the spot, you will sound worse than if your answer wasn't what they wanted to hear. The delivery is key here.

People trained to do behavioral interviews are looking for answers that show how you approached a situation and subsequently resolved it. The PAR and RAP sheets lend themselves perfectly to show this. The answers to behavioral questions differ only slightly from the ones that show skills, as you can see above. We slightly changed the skill based answer that we used in RAP example #1 to become a behavioral based answer which leans more toward showing the *competency* as opposed to the *skill*. It also tends to sound more like a story.

I recommend that you Google "behavioral interview questions" or "competency based interview questions" and it will give you a plethora of possible questions. Don't let them intimidate you. It would serve you well to read through them for familiarity and understanding of what kind of questions may come your way. Go through them and answer them with your background stories. Pick a few questions that represent each category and practice, practice, practice!

Being prepared for these questions has the ability to make you shine above the rest of the people being considered for this job. Make the list; do the work; prepare.

# Behavioral Based Competency Categories and Questions

There are lists upon lists of these categories and questions on the internet. Search for them and practice answering the questions. Here are many of the categories you will find and some of the questions you may be asked in a behavioral based interview.

CATEGORIES:

| | |
|---|---|
| Effective Communication | Ability to Learn |
| Problem Solving | Management |
| Leadership | Resilience |
| Analytical Skills | Risk Taking |
| Judgment | Team Player |
| Critical Thinking | Process Operation |
| Attention to Detail | Technical Knowledge |
| Decisiveness | Tenacity |
| Planning | Work Standards |
| Interpersonal Skills | Ethics |
| Delivering Results | Client Interface |
| Innovation | Handling Pressure |
| Fact Finding | Team Building |
| Entrepreneurial Skills | Sensitivity |
| Work Independently | Participation |
| Integrity | Organization |
| Adaptability/Flexibility | Conflict Management |
| Persuasiveness | Achieving Goals |
| Initiative | Control |
| Delegation | Negotiation |
| Vision | Motivation |
| Development of Subordinates | Time Management |

Think about everything that each category may mean. Communication means both the ability to understand what someone is saying to you as well as the ability to effectively communicate your ideas to others. Motivation may mean ability to motivate yourself or the ability to motivate others. Think of examples in all areas of each category.

Before getting in to the sample questions, I want to stress that there are so many ways of asking about your background in each of the categories listed above. You really do need to get on the internet and search for behavioral interview questions with your RAP and PAR sheets in hand and answer every one you can find. The following pages contain some sample questions.

QUESTIONS:

Describe a major change that happened while you were in a past position and how you adapted to that change.

Tell me of a time when you made a suggestion to improve the work in your organization.

Tell me what you do to keep your job/industry knowledge current.

Describe a time when you couldn't meet a goal or deadline. What did you do to correct or handle the problem?

What is the most competitive work situation you have experienced?

Tell me about a time when you disagreed with the team and how you handled it.

Have you ever had to handle a dispute between co-workers and how did you resolve it?

What is the riskiest decision you have made on the job and how did it turn out? What would you have done differently?

Give an example of a time when you used logic to solve a problem.

Describe a time when you had to analyze a situation and develop a plan.

Tell me of a time when you had to address an angry customer.

Describe a time when you showed too much initiative.

Describe a time when you did not communicate something well. How did you correct the situation?

Tell me about a time that you had to communicate a complex concept to someone.

What's the most important business decision you have made in the last year and what process did you use to make it?

Give an example of a time when a decision that you made didn't turn out well. What did you do to resolve it?

Tell me about how you train new employees.

What do you do when faced with an obstacle to an important project or goal?

Describe a time when you had to juggle several projects/tasks at once. What did you do to assure that each one got the needed attention?

Give an example of a time when you went above and beyond the call of duty.

Describe a time when you had to make an unpopular decision. How did you get everyone on board?

Tell me about an 'outside the box' idea or decision that you implemented and what were the results?

What was one of your most creative ideas? Where did it come from?

Tell me about a time when you were responsible for motivating co-workers. How did you go about doing it? What was the response?

Describe a challenging negotiation in which you were involved.

How do you decide what gets priority when scheduling your time?

Give an example of a time when you were able to persuade someone to see things your way.

How do you develop a project plan for a team? How do you choose your team?

Describe your presentation style. How do you go about planning for a presentation?

Talk about a time when stress tested your coping skills. What did you do to handle it?

What has been the most creative thing you've done to solve a problem? What was the result?

Tell me about a time when you were less than pleased with your performance.

What do you consider your most valuable assets in business? Describe how you use them to accomplish your job.

What is the most useful criticism you have ever received and how did you apply it to your work life?

Describe a time at work when you had to use significant self control.

Tell me about a time when you had to completely change directions in a project. How did you refocus?

Think about these questions (I know that most aren't in the form of a question; bear with me on the term). How can anyone tell you the correct answer to them without knowing your complete background? You alone have the answers already. If you do the exercises of the RAP and PAR sheets, you will have the answers to all of the questions that could possibly apply to you. Read these questions and the questions you find on the internet and dig deep to find something that may apply. Remember that you don't have to get paid for the experience to count. You may have lead a committee or a volunteer project in your child's school that required Planning, Leadership, Conflict Resolution, Adaptability, Time Management, and many other categories. Use those situations as examples as well. They, too, can show the competency as well as the skill.

# Covering Negatives

If the negative is that you don't have a particular skill or experience that they are looking for, there are ways to cover that. If asked if you have experience in certain areas and you don't, state that although you have no 'widget' experience, that 'widgets' have long been a personal area of interest and that you feel that you can be up to speed in the 'widget' world in a very short time. You may also say something like "Although I have no direct widget experience, I've done quite a bit of research due to my interest in the widget arena." Offer to do the research, take a class or maybe stay late the first few weeks to come up to speed in the areas that the manager feels you are lacking.

Maybe there is *something* you can draw from that is similar. Get creative here. I did not say lie about your experience; just get creative about it. Many times I would be interviewing someone to find out about their experience and I had to do quite a bit of digging, but we found relatable experience enabling me to sell them in to a company. Maybe they are asking you to do something with the accounting department and you did a similar function in the sales department. Then you can state, "Although I've never bought paper clips for the accounting department, I did buy them for the sales department and they were very pleased with the results." You get the drift.

If you don't have a degree, a certification or specific skills that you think you need to have, NEVER lie about having them. I've seen many companies who wanted a degree but didn't require it, fail to hire simply because of the LIE. I've had companies refuse to make offers to the top choice candidates because they lied, not because they didn't have a degree; they have told me as much. I've even seen the lie to have been found out after the hire was made, resulting in firing. Don't lie; 'nuff said!

Don't discount your school, volunteer and intern experience. You are far better off mentioning that experience if at all applicable instead of not mentioning it at the expense of not getting the job. You can say, "Yes I did a similar project as my thesis" or "I interned in a group that was working on a similar project." You can even use background facts such as "I volunteer at my church and work on that very accounting system." ANY experience, no matter how slight you might think it is, is better than the company thinking that you have no familiarity with it whatsoever. It is a common misconception that only paid experience counts. That is just not true.

Don't forget to include these things on a separate RAP sheet for any school, volunteer or intern experience. Have a place on your resume for "Additional Experience" which sounds better than "Volunteer Experience".

An interviewer can sometimes be looking for negatives by asking illegal questions. Some very innocent sounding questions can be illegal.

Do you have children?
Are you married?
Where do you live?

How much longer do you plan to work before you retire?
Can you get a sitter for work/travel on short notice?

Which of those questions are illegal? All of them. Do you simply say, "That's an illegal question"? Where will that get you? Hired? I doubt it. Yes it may be an illegal question, but unless you are prepared to forfeit this job, you may want to just answer it in some way. Would it be illegal to refuse to hire you because of telling them it's an illegal question? My guess is yes, but let's talk about reality, not legality. The reality may very well be that you want this job.

In the sitcom the Mary Tyler Moore show's first episode, she's interviewing with a very gruff newsman, Lou Grant. He asks her about her religion and marital status – some very illegal interview questions - and she says, "Mr. Grant, you can't legally ask me that." He leans down and gets right in her face and barks, "Are you gonna call a cop?" If you're not "gonna call a cop" then you'd better find some way around or through the question.

So how do you answer those types of questions? As vaguely as possible. For instance, the question of children could be answered by saying, "Children won't be a problem in my ability to travel." That answer could mean either you do OR don't have children, but it doesn't affect your ability to travel either way.

On marital status you could answer with, "My marital status won't affect my ability to perform my duties in this position." You aren't telling them what your marital status is, just how the status won't matter.

Some of these questions you may have to maneuver around. "Where do you live?" may very well be a question of ability to get to work on time or come in on short notice. Address it. Answer with, "I have no problem getting to work on time or coming in on short notice if that's your concern." If there is a different concern than this, they will probably address it then.

You can also try to get the question "revoked" by replying with, "Does this have any bearing on my getting the job?" It also is a good reply for the question of your maiden name or questions that are hard to be vague about. When they tell you that it doesn't have any bearing, simply ask them an unrelated question about the position to move past it. (See list of questions in the question section ahead)

Look up illegal interview questions on the internet. Do this to determine more about what the interviewer may be trying to find out, when possible and work to answer the probable objection rather than avoiding the question.

# Company Research

I t is very important to do company research. You should have an answer to the question "Why do you want to work for this company?" It may be an interest in a new direction they are taking or that they train or treat their employees well. Be able to show that you've got more of an interest in working there than just a cure for your unemployment.

Scour their web site. There is so much information available and nearly every company has a web site. Most have quite informative web sites. This can be a great source to get ideas to help tailor your resume and create pertinent questions for your interview. Don't make the mistake of reading only the first page of the site and reciting it back to the hiring manager when asked what you know about the company. You'll be just like the last person they interviewed and probably the next. Dig deeper.

You will likely find a job description on the site under employment opportunities. Take notes while looking at the web site. They can also be reviewed before each interview with the company. You may be interviewing with multiple companies at any given time. It is quite often hard to keep the information straight between these companies. I recommend a manila file folder for each company. Slip your notes in to the folder along with a copy of the resume you sent them. If you are working with multiple companies AND multiple resumes, you will want to review both before each interview.

If it is a smaller company without job descriptions on the web site, place a call to the hiring manager in the department and ask if you can get a copy of the job description. As head hunters, they would provide those to us. A written job description is an abundant source of information in your quest to match your experience to the job. If asked why you want the job description, let them know that you want to be able to highlight all of your pertinent background in the interview so that they can better determine your ability to execute the position. Put it in your own words if you like, but say much the same thing. "I wanted to better determine if my skills match this position" might be a shortened version. Try to get a job description before submitting your resume. This will enable you to more accurately tailor your resume to fit the position. You will sometimes get lucky and get someone 'chatty' on the phone. Be prepared to take notes on this call. This information and job description goes in the company file for later review.

Do you know anyone working for the potential employer? They can give you an insight into the company culture. They can be a great source of information about the people you will be interviewing with. They may know something about the position and why it is open. It is worth asking around to see if anyone you know knows anyone working for the company or who used to work for the company. Remember that some of this information will be fact and some opinion. If you have multiple people you can talk to who work for a company, you can get more than one viewpoint. Take notes on this too. Add it to your company file.

Go to the social networking sites such as Facebook, Linked In, MySpace, Plaxo and Tagged and you can connect to many past and present employees of the company who can be an excellent source of information. You may be surprised at who you know that can provide an introduction or even put in a good word for you at the company where you will be interviewing.

Get the names and titles of all of the people you will be interviewing with and do some research on each person. Again, go back to the many business networking sites to seek out information. That, coupled with any information shown on the company web site about the interviewer, their position and possibly *their* job description, can give you quite a bit of insight in to this person before the interview ever starts. This can go a long way in putting you at your ease. Remember, interviewers are people just like you.

# Just Prior to Your Interview

Some of the things I am going to say might sound like things that shouldn't have to be said, but I'm going to say them anyway.

Do a thorough review the night before the interview. Study the company file you've put together. Go over the resume that you sent to them. Review and study your background on your RAP and PAR sheets. Study the answers you've developed to potential questions based on what you know about the job description using both skill and behavioral based answers. Practice saying them out loud even if you have to lock yourself in the bathroom to get the privacy to do so. Role play with someone if you can; have them ask some of these anticipated questions. This will be especially helpful with behavior based questions, making them less intimidating when asked in the interview. You never know what hidden talents they are looking for so study over your entire work history, not just what you think they want to know about. Something seemingly insignificant may apply in a way you've never thought of.

When you are finished studying your prep info, put the directions to the company, clean copies of your resume and a list of names of people you will be meeting with in the left pocket of your portfolio. On the legal tablet, divide the page so you have a consistent place to put the list of things you *must* let them know about your background to match yourself to the position, a place for additional questions you would like to ask, but can put off to a later or more appropriate time and reminders of what to do or not to do in the interview. If you have a bad habit of being too loud, in the reminder section draw a megaphone and a big X over it to remind you not to talk too loud. If you tend to wave your hands around too much when talking, maybe you can draw a hand with one of those circles with the diagonal lines through it like on the no smoking sign to remind you not to wave your hands around. If you withdraw upon meeting people and tend not to smile much, draw a big curve like a smile to remind you to be friendly, smile and not be over serious. Being professional doesn't mean you have to be boring or serious. That often comes off as unfriendly and who wants to work with someone they think is unfriendly? Glance at this section occasionally to check yourself and make sure you are making the best impression. See the sample in the Examples and Exercises section.

Lay your clothes out the night before. You may have unsettled nerves the morning of the interview and you don't want to be trying to figure out what to wear or if you have a clean shirt or socks to wear with your suit.

Don't drink or stay up too late the night before the interview. You may think it's no big deal, but ask yourself how bad you want this job. Is it important enough to you to make a better impression than *any* of the other people they will see for this job? Remember, it's only the person who makes the BEST impression who will be asked to take the position. Don't take a chance of not being at your best and at the top of your game.

Get up in plenty of time to wake up thoroughly, relax a bit before the interview and to get there in plenty of time. It's important to not be cloudy-headed or feel anxious or rushed. This is a good time to review the information about the first impression, the impression of the senses.

Eat something before your interview, preferably protein. You can't be sure how long it will take and you don't want your stomach rumbling or getting a hunger headache. Don't eat so much that you will be sleepy, either. Stick a 'just in case' power bar in your car, purse or pocket. You may have time between interviewers or between interviews at companies when you just need a little something to stave away the hunger for another hour. Be prepared.

Take a good look in the mirror before you leave for the interview and double check your appearance. Smile. Relax. Take a few cleansing breaths, deep and long. Breathe in slowly and deeply, then breathe out slowly and completely.

If it's a cross town interview, you are better off getting to that side of town early and going to a coffee shop to wait an extra 30 minutes than to be caught in traffic and late for the interview. You can always review some more. If you find yourself late for some reason, call the company BEFORE the time that the interview was scheduled and let them know the circumstances. Don't call at the time the interview is scheduled to start. That's too late to be considered considerate.

Just before you walk in to the company, take another deep cleansing breath to relax. Remember all of the reasons that you are right for this position to bolster your confidence. You are well prepared at this point; more well prepared than the other candidates who also want this position. This should give you a well deserved feeling of confidence.

Walk in the door to the company 10 minutes before your interview time. More than 15 minutes sometimes puts a feeling of pressure on someone who may not be prepared to receive you 20-30 minutes before the interview time. They might feel rushed to finish what they are doing to get to your interview. Never give a reason for a negative feeling. Remember, feelings are a part of the first impression. If you arrive late, you've given the impression that this job is not important to you no matter how much you apologize.

# Controlling the Interview

Have you ever heard the expression that whoever is asking the questions is in control of the conversation? How true that is. But wait, if someone is interviewing you, how can you be the one who is asking the questions? I will show you a very effective way to switch roles right from the start without upsetting or offending the interviewer.

Allow the interviewer to ask the first question. If they are "fact" questions such as "What university did you attend?" or "How many years have you been with your current company?" then you can give an answer. Those usually won't be the first questions if your resume was provided before the interview. I find that people usually ask a very general question to start with such as "Tell me about yourself" or "Tell me about your experience or background." These are very broad requests for information.

Before I get in to how to turn this question around, let me say that this is a place where many people stumble. Some people will respond with way too much off topic and inappropriate information for an interview situation. I have heard people launch in to their sordid past, talk about everything that was wrong with their old job/company, talk about their current woes, and basically shoot themselves in the foot as far as getting the job. Don't make this mistake.

You can follow up the very general question regarding any portion of your background with, "I'd like to direct my response/answer to the specific skills and proficiencies you are looking for. What is most important for you to find in the person who will take this position?" Get the hiring authority talking about the ideal person who will fill this position. Try to get a feel for what matters most to him. This is when you will jot words that will jog your memory about parts of your background that apply to their needs. You will use some version of the answers you've prepared, showing the responsibilities you had in those areas, the actions you took to execute your responsibilities and the payoff for having successfully done so. Make sure you don't give a dissertation without checking in to see if you are overdoing it. After using the basic answer that it was a responsibility that you had, the actions you took and the result of your actions, ask, "Would you like to know more about the project?" or "Would you like to know more about my involvement in the project?" They might just need to know *that* you've done it, not every detail. It's like the old analogy – Don't tell someone how to build a clock if they only want to know what time it is.

Even if you have acquired a job description, there may be something on the description that they don't care if you have or not. If job descriptions are written by the Human Resource department, they may not reflect the hiring manager's needs accurately. There could be things they really would like to have in the way of experience that aren't listed on this description. You need to hear from the "horse's mouth" what truly matters.

Don't spend time talking their ear off about something that may not matter to them. It leaves less time for something else they may want to know about. If there are multiple people for you to see in the interview process, something different may matter to each of them. Be sure to ask EACH person what skills you can bring to the table that may help to make *their* job easier. The question can go like this, "What can I do in this position that will help support you in your position?" or "…support you and your department?" If you ask that question with an air of wanting to make their job easier, when asked for their input, who do you think that they will recommend for the position?

Giving information using what I call third party references is a very strong way to get your experience across. It accomplishes much. First, you are able to brag shamelessly without sounding cocky. If fact, it has the opposite effect if used correctly; it can make you sound great *and* humble. It also gives the feeling to the hiring authority that he's already received a reference of sorts on you and it's entirely favorable.

It goes like this. From time to time when telling your experience, do it through someone else's eyes. The manager may ask if you've ever hired people for a project. Your answer could be, "Yes, in fact my boss used to tell me I had a real knack for choosing the right people to be part of the project team." Question: "Can you work effectively with the computer users?" Answer: "I believe so. The users used to thank me for being so patient with them while training them on the new software." You will execute these answers with a very slight "awe shucks" demeanor. Too much of that becomes phony. Just think humility when you answer with third party references.

Play around with your RAP and PAR sheets and your answers to potential questions and put those answers in third party reference form. Think of someone that has commented on or complimented you and/or your abilities in any way. Remember that being assigned tasks because of your ability is a compliment from your boss. Compliments don't always start with "You're so good at…" Go down your list of responsibilities to look for more examples of people showing confidence in you through deeds as well as comments. That may sound like, "My boss always assigned me time critical tasks because he knows my projects run efficiently and always come in on time." It's a great exercise. There's an example and exercise in the Examples and Exercises section in the back of the book to work on your third party references.

# Questions to Ask in the Interview

Many people think you should wait until the end of the interview to ask questions. That's when the manager typically asks, "Do you have any questions?" Don't wait until the end of the interview to ask questions; by then it is too late for them to serve their purpose. Ask questions during the interview as a part of your discovery process. Questions get you the information you need to be able to demonstrate that you are the right person for the position.

Never ask a question you don't have a reason to ask. In other words, don't ask a question just to be asking a question. Your questions must have purpose. They must play in to the end result you are looking for in this interview which is to show that you are a perfect match for this job, resulting in an offer to you for the position. It is basically a match game. You pull out of them the information about what they are looking for and then feed it back to them in responses that demonstrate how you've done those things in your past jobs.

Some questions are for the department in which the position exists and some are for the human resource department. Some are for both. Generally speaking, ask questions about the company and the company direction from the human resource department. They are trained to "sell" the company to you. They can walk you through benefits and perks of working for the company at the appropriate time.

A first interview is not the time to address benefits, however. This is also not the time to ask comfort and convenience questions such as, "Do I get an office or will I be in a cube?", "Do we get headsets?" or, "How soon can I take a vacation day?" To paraphrase or *rephrase* the famous line from JFK's 1961 inaugural speech, when interviewing you must remember to "Ask not what the company can do for you, ask what you can do for the company!" The proper time to ask comfort, convenience and benefit questions is when you want the company AND the company wants you. That hasn't been determined until you've also met with the hiring authority in the department with the open position and they have expressed their interest in the form of an offer or at minimum a second interview and second HR interview to address benefits. Addressing benefits before the time is right can come across as a "what's in it for me" attitude and you want to give a "how can I be a valuable asset to the company" impression.

When you are interviewing with the department, try to finish the answer to some of their questions with an appropriate question that tells you something more about the job. This information is vital in matching your skills to the job. This is how that might sound:

*As a team lead for the analyst on our conversion project, I was responsible for making sure 'user needs' information was quickly and accurately provided to the development team. I asked the developer's team lead to meet with me to determine better and faster ways of getting user needs information to his team. As a result, the project came in ahead of time and under budget. **What type of project will I lead as my first assignment?***

Tacking on a question at the end of an answer lets you get those questions in there without having to wait for a break in the conversation or awkwardly throwing them in to the discussion randomly. We also did something else with the question tacked on to the answer here. We've placed ourselves in the job. This is something that you want to do throughout your interview. The question we added on could have been asked *after* getting the job.

Try to get to the pain of having this position unfilled. You want to know what pain you can relieve from the hiring manager. I can tell you that one of the pains he is feeling is having to go through the interview process. He would rather be doing his job, not interviewing. If you go in prepared for your interview in such a manner that he practically has to just sit back and listen to you get your *pertinent* background information across to him, he's going to love you already.

Get to what problems having this position unfilled are creating. Is there a backflow of paperwork that is going undone? Tout your ability to get it done efficiently *and* accurately. Is a project costing more due to lack of direction? Talk about your ability to lead effectively. Are sales being lost to other companies? Speak of your innovative marketing skills. What pain will be relieved when this job is filled by the right person? This is where you will target much of your questioning. Get the manager talking about what pain you can relieve for him. Then let him know how you can relieve his pain through stories of your background and accomplishments in past positions. This will demonstrate how your experience can help relieve his pain.

Here are some sample questions for you to ask. Based on the type of position and company, these questions can be reworded. These are only a few of the endless list of questions you could ask to gain information about the job. I recommend making a list of questions that would pertain to the specific types of jobs you may be looking at.

Sample Questions:

What is the first thing you would have me accomplish in this position?

What would be my first major project?

What problems are you looking for the person who takes this position to solve?

What problems will be solved by having this position filled?

What are some of the department/company goals and how can I help to achieve those goals?

What could the person who fills this spot do to make your job easier?

Why is this position open?

What is the skill or trait you most want to see in the person who fills this job?

How can I make an immediate impact on this company/department?

What is the most critical issue your department is addressing currently?

Why weren't the people who filled this position in the past right for it?

Why have people left this position in the past?

What additional responsibilities will come my way during the first year?

What do other candidates you are considering for this position lack?

When would you like to have this position filled by?

Is there anything that would keep me from being your first choice candidate?

Is there anything standing in the way of making me an offer?

# Closing the Interview

Before you leave the interview, you need to know that you have covered all concerns of the hiring manager with regard to your qualifications matching what he needs. It's great if you feel that you're the right person for the job, but that's not what will get you an offer. What will get you an offer is if HE feels that you are qualified for the position and feels that you are the right person for the job. Ask, in a very straightforward manner, "Do you feel I'm qualified for this position?" and if not, "In what areas do you feel I am not qualified?" Another way to ask might be, "Is there anything that keeps me from being your first choice candidate?" The second question might reveal if there is another candidate with more or better experience for the job. Make the words feel comfortable for you. You don't want to leave the interview thinking you did great and with the hiring manager thinking, "I wish he had some 'xyz' experience". Maybe you *do* have 'xyz' experience but didn't know he needed it and he failed to ask. This is where you have a last chance to correct any misunderstandings about your background and find out what he feels you lack for the job. Then cover it.

This is when you will check your list of points you need to cover for any items that still need to be addressed. You may be asked if there are any other questions and you can get these points in at that time. Be sure to get in there with, "I just wanted to mention that I do have the xyz experience you mentioned was important for this job. I worked with xyz in my last position for about six months."

Asking for the job is the same in sales lingo as asking for the sale. Many sales are lost by simply not asking for them just as a job may be lost because the last/next person showed more interest by asking for the job and you didn't. Even if you're not sure if you want the job, ask for the job. It is better to have an offer and respond that you want to "talk it over with my spouse" or "I'd like to think it over" than not to get the offer and decide later that you really do want the job. Be excited about the opportunity. You can't go back later and create the excitement of the moment. The time to be excited about the opportunity and ask for the job is NOW.

To ask for the job say something like, "I'm not sure what importance this has in your decision making process, but I really do want this position. I feel I have a lot to offer this company and it feels like a good fit to me." It helps if you do this just as you are standing up to leave and shaking his hand while you are asking. It makes a bigger impact like that because you are standing face to face connected to him by shaking hands and looking him directly in the eye. Someone who is enthusiastically asking for the job is considered more seriously than someone who just gets up and leaves the interview.

# Phone Interviews

Some companies and/or hiring managers like to start with a phone interview. Sometimes you are applying for a job out of the city or state and a phone interview is required before they are willing to incur the expense of bringing you to town for a face to face interview. Some managers just want to save time by weeding out the people who aren't right for the job.

The same interview techniques apply in the phone interview as in the face to face interview. Make sure you have done your prep work and reviewed your background, the company *and* the person who will be doing the phone interview.

Here are a few tips for phone interviews. Prepare with a background review just as you would for a face to face interview. Even though you can have better access to your notes because you aren't sitting in front of the hiring manager, you don't want the sound of papers rattling in the background each time you answer a question.

Place or receive the call from a land line. You don't want a dropped call while trying to drive home an important point. Place or be there to receive the call ON TIME.

If you are slouching on the sofa wearing your bathrobe, you are going to sound like a guy sitting on the sofa in his bathrobe. You don't have to put on a suit, but be dressed; it does make a difference in your delivery. I find it best to be sitting up straight at a table or desk. You sound even better if you are standing up. Smile from time to time while you are talking; you will sound friendlier.

Have a glass of water within reach. Have a throat lozenge handy. If you get a sudden tickle in your throat you won't have to hack and cough in the manager's ear. Pop in a lozenge until you feel the tickle has passed and take it out so you sound clear. Other than that, don't chew on candy or gum during the phone interview.

Make sure that your phone is operating properly. Make a call to someone to check that the phone reception is clear. Take this important call in private with no TV or radio on in the background. Make sure you are away from barking dogs and crying kids. You want to be in a silent, private place.

The goal of a phone interview is to get a face to face interview. Ask for the interview at the end of the conversation. For instance, "If you feel I may be right for this position, I'd like to set an interview as soon as it's convenient for you." If you don't get an agreement for a face to face interview, ask what the manager feels you are lacking to be considered for the job. It may be something you do have experience with but haven't mentioned. Just like when you are leaving a face to face interview, you want to know what might be keeping you from being considered for this job so you can cover the objection.

# The Follow Up

Following up after the interview is very important. You want to be on the hiring manager's mind. Start with a thank you note for the interview. This is a way to reiterate your appropriate experience and further clear up any misunderstandings about your background or experience. This is the time to address the skills that they think you might be missing for this job. This is where you will once again ask for the job. Below is a sample thank you letter. Be sure to write one to each of the people you interviewed with; key in on the things that were important to each of these people.

*Dear Hiring Manager,*

*Thank you for the time you took to explore my background. I enjoyed our discussion of your plans to expand your sales force. I feel that I have much to bring to the table in the development of your force. My previous positions have prepared me well to accomplish this task.*

*You were concerned about my medical background being in a different sector. I feel that my sales team building ability will be the key factor in successfully expanding your team. I also didn't have the specific medical equipment experience when I came in to make XYZ Medicals the number one medical equipment seller in the entire state.*

*Once again, know that my interest level is extremely high and that I truly want to be part of building the ABC Medical sales team.*

*Sincerely,*

*Perfect Candidate*

You can see that not only did we thank him for the interview, we kept ourselves on his radar. We also took the opportunity to cover a concern that the hiring manager raised in the lack of experience with the exact type of medical equipment they sell; we hit home that important point with a past success. It may be experience or a success you forgot to mention when you were in the interview or one that you did mention that just bears repeating because of his concern.

If your handwriting is at all legible, hand write the thank you note on a blank note card or blank thank you card. It is more personal. Type it only if you have to. Even though this should be hand written, it would serve you well to quickly type it in to a word document not only as a record and future reference for other letters, but there is one other important reason. It is extremely bad to send a letter to a desired future employer with misspellings. It can truly cost you the job; I've seen it happen – DO A SPELLCHECK! Make sure you also have the correct spelling of the names of the people you are sending thank you notes to.

Sometimes there is not time to mail a letter and get it there before the decision is to be made. Keep these thank you notes handy. Hand deliver the notes the next day and ask the receptionist or assistant to see that they are delivered to the people you interviewed with. If you mail them, mail them the SAME DAY as the interview so they are received quickly. Keep note cards and stamps handy.

# Talking Money & Negotiating the Salary

Talking about money isn't always easy. It's a subject that you are emotionally tied to. As a general rule, I tell people that he who talks money first loses. If someone asks you how much you are making or have made in your previous positions, you should tell them. If you have a tiered compensation package, you can say "my package with salary and bonuses is/was worth $75,000 per year."

If you are asked what salary you would take for the position, you should reply, "I'm open to consider your best offer." or "I'd very much like to entertain any offer that you feel is commensurate with my skill level." You can play with the wording and have several similar sentences to pull out depending on which one feels most comfortable in any given situation. Sometimes you have to use a few of them while tap dancing around the money issue. They may ask a second time and you can answer with a different practiced sentence that says basically the same thing. Another good response when asked for a second time is, "I'd really like to know what you think my skill set is worth." or "…is worth to you and your company." This approach works best for smaller and some mid-sized companies, possibly even some larger companies.

For larger companies and companies with more structured organizational charts, there are usually pay grades for each position that have bottom, mid and high end ranges. Generally the company likes to bring people on board in the low to mid range. They want to leave room for raises while in this position. There are also internal equity issues at play. If they have a five year guy making 50K and you are a 5 year guy requiring 55K, they can't justify paying you more than their current employee at the same level.

When answering the money question of what you would take for the job with larger companies with pay grades, the best responses might sound more like, "Understanding my current compensation (or my skill level, experience level etc.), where do I fit into this position's pay grade?"

Have in mind a good idea of what you would take in compensation for any given position you are interviewing for *before* the offer is actually made. If you have someone to discuss the offer with, discuss it before hand. If an offer is made and it is what you would happily take for the position, accept the position on the spot. It not only shows decisiveness, it also shows how much you want to work for the company. A job offer is kind of like a marriage proposal, there's a big difference in a yes right away and a "can I think about it overnight?" Even if the answer is yes the next day, which answer would make you feel more desired? The company is proposing to you; if the job and offer are acceptable to you, say yes.

If negotiations are needed to get the offer to an acceptable level, try not to be the one to throw out the first number. Once you've given an amount, you can't really negotiate up from there. Don't give a specified amount. You could say, "I really feel that my skill level matches this position well. Would you consider a higher offer?" You could also ask, "What skills would you want to make a higher offer?" You may be able to negotiate a review for a raise if the skill is acquired by a specified time. "If I became proficient in that skill in three months, would you consider a review for a raise at that time?" If they say they can't make a better offer, you can still accept the original offer if you want it.

Play with possible offer scenarios in your head before the interview. Know what amount you would take and at what point you would walk away from the position. This will truly help to make your negotiating and decision making at the time of the offer much easier.

# Conclusion

Considering that you are qualified, preparation is the key to being the number one candidate for any job. Remember the saying, "Close only counts in horseshoes and hand grenades"? Close to being the first choice is not going to get you the job. Only *being* the first choice candidate will get you the job. What will make you the first choice is preparation, preparation and more preparation. I lived by this credo during my years as a top producing headhunter. My candidates blew the others out of the water nearly every time. When I left headhunting to address some health issues, I received many calls from other headhunters asking me to meet with them and teach them to prepare their candidates the way I did. Many told me they didn't get their hopes up when they knew their candidates were going up against mine.

My advice to you would be to take this interview process seriously. I would typically refuse to work with a job candidate who would not take their job search seriously enough to do the preparation. I would ask them, "If you don't care that much about your job search then why should I?" I worked on commission. I only got paid if the candidate got the job. I wanted the manager to be drooling over my candidates so I learned to prepare them well and it not only made me a lot of money, it gained me local, statewide and national recognition. A candidate's unwillingness to do the work to prepare for an interview spoke volumes to me. I ask the same question I use to ask my candidates to you now in another way, "Do you care enough about getting the offer to be more prepared that the other candidates?" The *true* answer is yes *only* if you do the preparation.

The preparation process is a formula. It's a simple formula but does take some work. Your desire for being hired has to be stronger than your desire to avoid the preparation. I encourage you to reread this book while working through the steps I've outlined for you.

I hope you take the time to apply these concepts and work through the exercises. I feel that if you have multiple interviews, you will more than likely have multiple offers as my candidates so often did. And isn't that a better place to be in than wishing for an offer that never comes?

Happy interviewing!

I've seen many books that claim to be able to give you answers to interview questions. How can that be? How can someone know your background? Without intimate knowledge of your background these answers can be vague and general at best. How will that give the hiring manager the information about you he needs to make an informed decision? Only you have the knowledge of every detail of your work experience.

Study the examples laid out for you and work through the exercises. You can't know the exact questions that will be asked in the interview. What you *can* do is organize and study your background information in a way that allows you to deliver it effectively. That is what these exercises are all about.

Interview Note Page

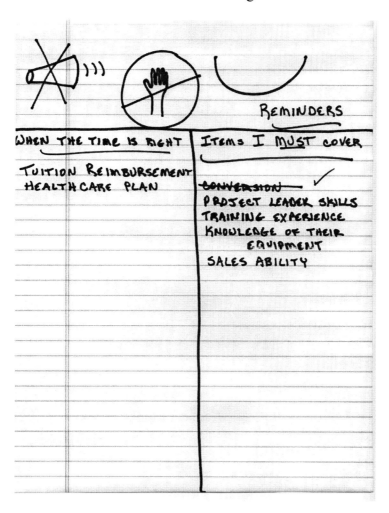

## List of Responsibilities in Reverse Chronological Order

_____
_____
_____
_____
_____
_____
_____
_____
_____
_____
_____
_____
_____
_____
_____
_____
_____
_____
_____
_____
_____
_____
_____
_____
_____
_____
_____
_____
_____
_____
_____

## List of Responsibilities in Reverse Chronological Order

## List of Responsibilities in Reverse Chronological Order

_____
_____
_____
_____
_____
_____
_____
_____
_____
_____
_____
_____
_____
_____
_____
_____
_____
_____
_____
_____
_____
_____
_____
_____
_____

## List of Responsibilities in Reverse Chronological Order

| RESPONSIBILITY | ACTION | PAYOFF |
|---|---|---|
| Lead a team of analysts to determine user needs and deliver the information to the development team. | Initiated a meeting with the lead from the development team to coordinate efforts and speed up the flow of information between the groups. | The development project came in on time and under budget due to there being no lag time in gathering and delivering user needs to the developers. |
| Development of new clients. | Created an industry newsletter and distributed it among targeted potential and existing clients. | Quickly considered an industry 'expert' because of my editorials in the newsletters. Clients took my calls more readily and tended to do business with me over their other sources. |
| Coordinate schedules for 3 VPs including meetings and travel. | Lined up contacts with several caterers for the meetings and two highly recommended travel agents to handle the travel with a simple phone call. | Even last minute meetings and travel were all able to be handled quickly and with ease. |
| Increase revenues at our retail locations. | Designed a customer survey to determine what additional goods & services they would like to see at our store locations. | Added two products and one service that increased revenues by 15% within the next 6 months. |

Take a recent responsibility that you have seen through to an end and list it on the practice RAP sheet below. Fill in the action and payoff sections then turn it in to a polished sentence/answer.

| Responsibility | Action | Payoff |
|---|---|---|
|  |  |  |

Sentence/Answer:

_____

_____

_____

_____

_____

| RESPONSIBILITY | ACTION | PAYOFF |
|---|---|---|
| | | |

| RESPONSIBILITY | ACTION | PAYOFF |
| --- | --- | --- |
| | | |

| RESPONSIBILITY | ACTION | PAYOFF |
|---|---|---|
| | | |

| RESPONSIBILITY | ACTION | PAYOFF |
| --- | --- | --- |
| | | |

Sample PAR Sheet

| PROBLEM/PROFICIENCY | ACTION | RESULT |
|---|---|---|
| I was chosen to lead an accounting project because of my ability to complete projects with limited time frames. | Chose 3 people for the team who had worked on the same fiscal budget project the year prior.<br><br>Added a junior member to take care of less critical tasks.<br><br>Incentivized the team with a half-day off the Friday following an on time project completion. | Work was streamlined by having a junior team member to give lower level tasks to. This person also now has fiscal budget experience.<br><br>The project moved more efficiently due to using people with past experience in fiscal budget planning.<br><br>A junior accountant gained experience on the annual fiscal budget project.<br>The project came in on time. |

Categories: Management, Team Building, Time Management, Strategy, Developing Subordinates, Planning.

Answer/Story:

I was chosen to lead a team of accountants on the annual fiscal budget project because of my ability to complete projects that had limited time constraints. I chose a 4 person team consisting of 3 members with past fiscal budget project experience and one junior accountant who took care of less critical tasks. I took many of their current duties and assigned them to others in the accounting department for the duration of the project. These things helped to streamline the work and allowed the team to focus on getting the project done. This strategy also gave an additional person in the accounting department with fiscal budget experience.

## List of Problems/Proficiencies in Reverse Chronological Order

## List of Problems/Proficiencies in Reverse Chronological Order

_____
_____
_____
_____
_____
_____
_____
_____
_____
_____
_____
_____
_____
_____
_____
_____
_____
_____
_____
_____
_____
_____
_____
_____
_____
_____
_____
_____

## List of Problems/Proficiencies in Reverse Chronological Order

## List of Problems/Proficiencies in Reverse Chronological Order

_____
_____
_____
_____
_____
_____
_____
_____
_____
_____
_____
_____
_____
_____
_____
_____
_____
_____
_____
_____
_____
_____
_____
_____
_____
_____
_____
_____
_____
_____

| PROBLEM/PROFICIENCY | ACTION | RESULT |
| --- | --- | --- |
|  |  |  |

| PROBLEM/PROFICIENCY | ACTION | RESULT |
| --- | --- | --- |
| | | |

| PROBLEM/PROFICIENCY | ACTION | RESULT |
|---|---|---|
| | | |

| PROBLEM/PROFICIENCY | ACTION | RESULT |
| --- | --- | --- |
| | | |

# Third Party Reference Examples

Refer back to the sample RAP and PAR sheets. We will use these items to formulate examples of third party references as follows:

From the RAP sheet…

1. I was assigned an ongoing project that was having trouble. My boss told me that he wanted me to take over because of my problem solving and time management skills. He said he knew he could count on me to get the project on track, which I did.

2. My coworkers loved that my editorials brought the company 'industry expert' status and gained us new business.

3. My boss has complimented me more than once on how efficiently I plan his meetings and events.

4. The sales people have thanked me for bringing increased revenues through new products, helping to raise their commissions.


From the PAR sheet…

1. The less experienced team member I chose to work on the budget told me how much he appreciated gaining the additional experience. He said it would really help in his career development.

Go back through your RAP and PAR sheets and develop each one in to a third party reference. You won't use each one as a third party reference during the interview, but it's a great exercise. It can make a big difference if you have done this exercise because you never know which one will be appropriate to use until you are in the actual interview. The exercise is good preparation. You can also blend these third party references in to your complete answers to some behavioral and skill based questions. Practice on the next few pages.

Third Party Reference Exercise

There are many ways to begin the statements that give third party references. A few examples might be:

I've received many compliments about my ability to...

My coworkers have said…

My boss always chooses me to/for _____ because of my ability to…

My clients like that I…

I've been thanked for...

I've been told that…

My boss says that I…

Try some of these (and a few of your own) below:

_____

_____

_____

_____

_____

_____

_____

_____

_____

_____

_____

_____

_____

_____

_____

_____

_____

## Third Party Reference Worksheet

# Third Party Reference Worksheet

_____
_____
_____
_____
_____
_____
_____
_____
_____
_____
_____
_____
_____
_____
_____
_____
_____
_____
_____
_____
_____
_____
_____
_____
_____
_____
_____
_____
_____

## Third Party Reference Worksheet

# About the Author...

Sandy Scardino began a sales career in the 80's. She successfully became the top producer at both sales companies she worked for until finding her niche in headhunting in 1989. She soon became the top producer in the firm where she remained for ten years.

Her awards and accolades are many. She was a Top Ten Producer in the Houston Area Association of Personnel Consultants' Technical and Professional Division garnering seven consecutive Top Ten/Outstanding Achievement awards including the HAAPC #2 producer award, second only to the owner of the company she worked for.

She won as many awards on the Texas state level where she ranked near the top of the Top Fifteen Producer/Outstanding Achievement list's Technical and Professional Division for each of the seven years she was eligible. Sandy took on the training at the firm she worked for, providing weekly training sessions for both rookie and seasoned recruiters.

Her consistency in being a Top Producer in her industry gained her acceptance into the prestigious Pinnacle Society, a consortium of 75 of the top headhunters in the United States. To qualify you must have had $1,000,000 in personal production in three years with one year totaling over $400,000 and the other two over $300,000, which she did with ease.

Visit the web site at www.ACINGTHEINTERVIEW.com for information on private interview coaching, group classes and downloadable forms.

LaVergne, TN USA
22 September 2010
198060LV00001B/102/P